I dare you

Story written by Gill Munton
Illustrated by Tim Archbold

Speed Sounds

Consonants *Ask children to say the sounds.*

f	l	m	n	r	s	v	z	sh	th	ng
ff	ll	mm	nn	rr	ss	ve	zz			nk
ph	le	(mb)	kn	wr	se		se			
					c		s			
					(ce)					

b	c	d	g	h	j	p	qu	t	w	x	y	ch
bb	k	dd	gg		g	pp		tt	wh			tch
	ck				ge							

Each box contains one sound but sometimes more than one grapheme.
*Focus graphemes for this story are **circled**.*

Vowels

Ask children to say the sounds in and out of order.

a	e ea	i	o	u	ay a-e	ee ea y e	igh i-e ie i	ow o-e o
at	hen	in	on	up	day	see	high	blow

oo u-e ue	oo	ar	or oor ore aw	air are	ir ur er	ou ow	oy oi
zoo	look	car	for	fair	whirl	shout	boy

Story Green Words

Ask children to read the words first in Fred Talk and then say the word.

Radar Rob   Cosmic Clare   spare   dare   bare   huge   eyes*

Ask children to say the syllables and then read the whole word.

com|pare   chick|en   fan|fare   cra|ter   no|tice   nos|trils

re|pro|gram   soft|ware   re|pair

Ask children to read the root first and then the whole word with the suffix.

scare → scared   sprint → sprinted   declare → declared

bulge → bulging   flare → flared   peep → peeped

glare → glared

* Challenge Words

Vocabulary Check

Discuss the meaning (as used in the story) after the children have read each word.

	definition:	sentence:
prepare	get ready	*Prepare to be very, very scared.*
sprinted	ran fast	*She peeled off her green skin, and sprinted off.*
compare	decide what is the same between two things	*"You can't compare that with running round the astroschool bare!"*
chicken	coward	*"Chicken!" shouted Clare.*
declared	said, promised	*"I'll get you back for that, Clare!" declared Rob.*
crater	hole in the ground	*She pointed to a small crater with a notice pinned to the rim.*

Red Words

two	there	who	were
you	said	your	one
could	what	was	school
to	of	all	should
want	does	through	many

I dare you

There's a lot of spare time in space,
and the kids who live up there often get bored.

Like the time on Planet Zox when Radar Rob
(square blue body, six yellow legs, pointed head)
and Cosmic Clare (small, green, round)
were kicking a spaceball on the stairs
before astroschool one day ...

"Let's play 'I dare you'," said Clare.
"You start."

"Okay," said Rob.
"Prepare to be very, very scared, Clare.
I dare you to …

… peel off your green skin,
and run round the astroschool – bare!"

"I'm not scared!" said Clare.
She peeled off her green skin, and sprinted off.

"I've got a good one for you, Rob," said Clare as she stepped back into her skin. "I dare you to ...

... put on a pair of moonboots – no, you'll need three pairs, Rob – and climb to the top of the radar mast!"

"That's not fair!" said Rob.
He glared at Clare.
"You can't compare that with running round the astroschool bare!"

"Chicken!" shouted Clare. So off Rob went.

"I'll get you back for that, Clare!" declared Rob.
"I dare you to …

stand on a chair and play a fanfare
on your rocket-boosted trumpet,
throwing your space hat in the air at the same time."

Clare stared at him.

"You look a bit green, Clare," said Rob.

"I always do!" Clare replied, reaching for her trumpet.

"You're not going to like this one, Rob," said Clare.
"I dare you to …

… go in there!"

She pointed to a small crater with a notice pinned to the rim.
The notice said, "Beware of the robodog!"

Two huge hairy paws rested on the rim of the crater.
Two bulging yellow eyes glared at Rob. Two red nostrils flared.

"Take care!" said Clare.

Clare couldn't see what happened next. But there was a lot of noise.

"Woof!" "Crash!" "Clank!" "Woof–woof!" "Boff!" "Help!"

Then Rob's pointed face (fairly red) peeped
out of the crater, followed by his six yellow legs (a bit bent).

There was a big hole in his
square body, and his chest was
making a ticking sound.

"Are you all right?" asked Clare.

"No, I'm not!
I'll have to reprogram all my software!"
said Rob, reaching inside his chest.

"I'll help to repair you," said Clare.
"And you can share my Star Bar if you like."

"Okay," said Rob.
"That seems fair. Just one more thing – no more games of 'I dare you'!"

Questions to talk about

Ask children to TTYP each question using 'Fastest finger' (FF) or 'Have a think' (HaT).

p.9 (FF)   What were Radar Rob and Cosmic Clare doing before astroschool one day?

p.10 (FF)   Where did Cosmic Clare have to run while she was bare?

p.11 (FF)   What did Cosmic Clare call Radar Rob when he didn't want to do the dare?

p.12 (FF)   How many things did Cosmic Clare have to do at once?

p.13 (FF)   What did the notice pinned to the crater say?

p.14 (HaT) How was Rob injured when he came out of the crater?

p.15 (HaT) Why do you think Rob didn't want to play any more games of 'I dare you'?

Questions to read and answer

(Children complete without your help.)

1. Why can it be boring in space?

2. What is Rob's first dare to Clare?

3. Why does Rob say Clare's dare is not fair?

4. What does the robodog look like?

5. Why do you think giving dares is not a good thing?

Speedy Green Words

Ask children to practise reading the words across the rows, down the columns and in and out of order clearly and quickly.

space	climb	round	same
often	chair	prepare	hairy
square	beware	green	before
prepare	care	start	play
scare	time	very	throwing